BEING FEMALE **IN AMERICA**

MALE PRIVILEGE

BY DUCHESS HARRIS, JD, PHD
WITH HEIDI DEAL

Essential Library

An Imprint of Abdo Publishing | abdopublishing.com

Published by Abdo Publishing, a division of ABDO, PO Box 398166, Minneapolis, Minnesota 55439. Copyright © 2018 by Abdo Consulting Group, Inc. International copyrights reserved in all countries. No part of this book may be reproduced in any form without written permission from the publisher. Essential Library™ is a trademark and logo of Abdo Publishing.

Printed in the United States of America, North Mankato, Minnesota
092017
012018

Cover Photo: Shutterstock Images
Interior Photos: iStockphoto, 4–5, 10–11, 30, 46, 53, 58–59, 73; Aleksandar Nakic/
iStockphoto, 9; Richard Levine/Alamy, 14–15; Robert Stolarik/Polaris/Newscom,
17; Antonio Guillem/iStockphoto, 22; Shutterstock Images, 26–27; Agence Opale/
Alamy, 33; Uber Images/Shutterstock Images, 36–37; Dusan Petkovic/Shutterstock
Images, 41; Diego Cervo/iStockphoto, 48–49; Money Business Images/Shutterstock
Images, 56, 78; Dasha Petrenko/Shutterstock Images, 62–63; Lucas Jackson/AP
Images, 66; Alexander Raths/Shutterstock Images, 70–71; Katarzyna Bialasiewicz/
iStockphoto, 80–81; Patti McConville/Alamy, 85; Gavin Rodgers/Alamy, 87; Splash
News/Newscom, 91; Kevin Dietsch/UPI/Newscom, 92–93; Terrence Jennings/Polaris/
Newscom, 98–99

Editor: Alyssa Krekelberg
Series Designer: Maggie Villaume

PUBLISHER'S CATALOGING-IN-PUBLICATION DATA

Names: Harris, Duchess, author | Deal, Heidi, author.
Title: Male privilege / by Duchess Harris and Heidi Deal.
Description: Minneapolis, Minnesota : Abdo Publishing, 2018. | Series: Being female
     in America |
Identifiers: LCCN 2017946731 | ISBN 9781532113079 (lib.bdg.) | ISBN 9781532151958
     (ebook)
Subjects: LCSH: Sexism--Juvenile literature. | Masculinity--United States--Juvenile
     literature. | Social history--Juvenile literature.
Classification: DDC 305.32--dc23
LC record available at https://lccn.loc.gov/2017946731

CONTENTS

CHAPTER ONE

WHAT IS
MALE PRIVILEGE?

In 1776, a group of men from all 13 colonies gathered to discuss the Declaration of Independence. In the beginning of the Declaration, Thomas Jefferson wrote, "We hold these truths to be self-evident, that all men are created equal, that they are endowed by their Creator with certain unalienable Rights."[1] It is with this one sentence that a group of men continued the patriarchal traditions that were carried over from Europe. Women were excluded from political affairs because they were believed to be less competent than men. No women were present to review the document to ensure their equal rights and freedoms would be guaranteed.

In the early years of American society, wives were considered the property of their husbands. They weren't allowed to vote, except for some wealthy women who owned property. Usually this meant that the woman inherited the

"REMEMBER THE LADIES"

Abigail Adams wrote a letter to her husband, John, while he was on his way to join the Continental Congress to review the Declaration of Independence: "In the new code of laws which I suppose it will be necessary for you to make, I desire you would Remember the Ladies and be more generous and favorable to them than your ancestors. Do not put such unlimited power into the hands of the Husbands. Remember, all Men would be tyrants if they could. If particular care and attention is not paid to the Ladies, we are determined to foment a Rebellion, and will not hold ourselves bound by any Laws in which we have no voice or Representation." John replied, "As to your extraordinary code of laws, I cannot help but laugh."[2]

property when her husband died, as married women couldn't own property in their own right. Women were limited in their options to get a formal education. Most white women were expected to stay home and care for the house and children. Men had the freedom to seek employment, enjoy social time with friends, receive an education, and participate in government.

The lack of rights these women had is an extreme example of male privilege. The concept of male privilege is frequently discussed in American society today, but what is it? It's an invisible set of benefits favoring the male population in the United States. These invisible benefits cover most aspects of a man's everyday life, including social life, politics, the workplace, and education. Male privilege

CONFRONTING PRIVILEGE

In the 1980s, Peggy McIntosh, a women's studies academic at Wellesley College in Massachusetts, was leading a seminar. She asked how each academic discipline could be changed by recognizing women. Male faculty noted that while they enjoyed learning about women's studies, their syllabi were already full. One man said, "When you are trying to lay the foundation blocks of knowledge, you can't put in the soft stuff." McIntosh liked these men. But this experience made her realize that these men could be both nice and oppressive. She noted, "These are nice men. But they're very good students of what they've been taught, which is that men make knowledge." In 1988, McIntosh wrote a paper titled *White Privilege and Male Privilege: A Personal Account of Coming to See Correspondences through Work in Women's Studies.* The paper laid out various situations of privilege and helped bring attention to the subject.[3]

does not require that a man ask for special benefits. Rather, the benefits of male privilege are so ingrained in American society that there is a natural bias in favor of men. This stems from the strong foundations of the male-dominated society on which America began.

The concept of male privilege is subjective, and it's often based on individual experience or perspective. There is no concrete, factual evidence that clearly defines the lines of male privilege. Instead, much of the debate is based on individuals' opinions, stereotypes, and generalizations. But there are obvious behaviors directed at women that consistently place them in a lower position in society and assign them a lower overall value in comparison with men.

TODAY'S PRIVILEGE

Male privilege presents itself in diverse ways and in different settings. It can sometimes go unrecognized because people are raised to accept the social norms that Americans have been living by for many years. One example of a common social norm includes expecting women to assume the bulk of household chores and childcare, even when those women work full-time jobs like their husbands. Men rarely face these pressures.

In 2015, more than one-third of working women had children under the age of 18.

Privilege for women has come a long way over the years. Today, women can pursue an education at nearly any college and seek out the career of their choice. They can vote and be elected into government positions. But evidence of male privilege exists in the very government of the United States, where most of the elected officials are men. The representation of women in these leadership roles is still limited.

There is a bias that gives men the upper hand, and it is formed and perpetuated by American society. One of the major indicators of male privilege is the struggle to close the wage gap between men and women. The wage gap is the difference in the amount of money men and women earn at full-time jobs. As of 2015, women earned less than 80 percent of what men made each year as full-time employees.[4] The wage gap makes it more difficult for women in the workforce to provide for their families. It also reduces the amount of money they will receive in retirement, because they earn less over their years in the workforce. In part because of the pay gap, there are more women in the United States living in poverty than men.

DISBELIEF OF MALE PRIVILEGE

Disbelievers of male privilege argue that men are the ones who must work harder and overcome more obstacles in American society, and that women are the ones who face less pressure. They speak of situations that show unfair treatment of men, such as the high percentage of male deaths in military combat and the low percentage of men who win custody of their children

Even when men and women are equally qualified and hold the same position at work, men receive higher pay on average.

SEXISM IN VIDEO GAMES

after a divorce. People use these examples and instances of stereotyping to argue that instead of male privilege, there is female privilege.

The lack of gender equality for both men and women in America plays a heavy role in how people shape their lives. For example, men are pressured to provide for their families and suppress their emotions to meet the standard ideal for a typical man. And although these examples are not fair to men, they are not examples of female privilege, says Nikita Redkar, an author at *Everyday Feminism*. "Women are not inherently benefiting from what men are disadvantaged by," she says. "The advantages women are thought to have at the expense of men reflect the patriarchy's demands for men as competitive, dominant, and authoritative. At the same time, its demands for women are to be submissive, nurturing, and inferior."[5]

But male privilege isn't the same for every man. And it's often credited as having a racial bias of its own. White men, for example, are more likely to reap the benefits of male privilege than black men. Gay men are less likely to enjoy the same male privilege benefits when they exhibit more feminine behaviors and characteristics, such as higher-pitched voices. There are intersections, though. A gay white male may reap more of the benefits than a black or Hispanic male.

It's not men's fault that there are a multitude of ways they benefit in American society at the expense of women. It is a result of a male-dominated culture. But understanding the privilege an individual has is the first step to initiating change toward true gender equality.

DISCUSSION STARTERS

- Have you ever experienced a situation firsthand in which male privilege was evident? Explain what happened.
- Can you think of examples of male privilege that are present in the media?
- Why would the Founding Fathers writing the Declaration of Independence deny women the rights they were demanding for themselves?

CHAPTER TWO

IT'S A
MAN'S WORLD

In American society, many things show favor toward men. Movies and television often put male characters in the spotlight, giving them the leading roles. Women play background characters such as assistants who ask a lot of questions, frazzled moms, and single women who are struggling to find the right man. In the business world, companies are overwhelmingly run by male CEOs. And a lot of advertising turns women into objects of men's desire. These are just some examples of how women and men are treated differently. Even when it might appear that women are benefiting from specialized treatment, such as in acts of chivalry, women are put on an unequal playing field in a submissive position.

STREET HARASSMENT

One way men and women are treated differently is in how their facial expressions are perceived. Men are rarely expected to smile when they speak or interact with others. Women, on the other hand, are expected to smile. If she isn't smiling, the woman will likely be labeled as cold, stuck-up, surly, or mean. This is one example of how society shows favor toward the male gender: women are responsible for providing comfort to men and seeking their approval, even if they are strangers.

An art series by Tatyana Fazlalizadeh called "Stop Telling Women to Smile" addresses gender-based street harassment. Gender-based street harassment toward women includes whistles, shouted comments such as "Hey, baby," and other unwanted comments from men, such as "Why aren't you smiling? Come over here, I'll make you happy."

The art series is placed outside in public spaces, with posters plastered on street poles and on walls along city streets. Artwork includes drawn portraits of women with captions that speak directly to offenders. Captions include phrases such as "My worth extends far beyond my body," "Men do not own the streets," "My outfit is not an invitation," and "Women are not outside for your entertainment."[1] "Stop Telling Women to Smile" challenges the privileged male perception that women are present simply for men's entertainment and pleasure.

DIFFERENCES IN BEHAVIOR

Male privilege can be identified in expectations of male and female behavior. Males are less likely to be criticized when they engage in unruly behavior. Using bad language, getting in fights, being disrespectful, and not following directions can be falsely attributed to natural instincts men are born with. Women, on the other hand, are expected to bite their tongues, not express their opinions or defend themselves, and do as they are told. Women who demonstrate the same behavior as men are considered out of control and are reprimanded or punished for not fitting in with societal norms. Men are granted the privilege of not being held accountable for certain behaviors, whereas women are held responsible for the same behaviors.

One area in which this double standard for males and females materializes is in situations involving angry outbursts. People accept a man's display of anger by minimizing it as an acceptable character trait. However, when a woman has an angry outburst, the immediate reaction from many people is that she is either overreacting or that the outburst is a result of her hormones. This difference in mind-set was confirmed in a 2008 study by Victoria Brescoll and Eric Uhlmann. The study showed that both male and female evaluators rated angry women as less professional and less valuable than angry men. Brescoll and Uhlmann noted that this response is because "public expressions of emotion are governed by strongly gendered social rules. Violating those rules can evoke negative reactions from others."[2] They also discovered that when men display anger, people perceive them as responding to an external situation. But when women display anger, people blame the woman and assume she is a naturally angry person.

INAPPROPRIATE BEHAVIOR EXCUSED

Shortly before the 2016 presidential election, the media leaked tapes of Republican candidate Donald Trump speaking about women in demeaning and inappropriate ways. He talked about grabbing women, and stated that he just goes up to women and kisses them. His wife, Melania, issued a statement saying, "The words my husband used are unacceptable and offensive to me. This does not represent the man that I know. I hope people will accept his apology, as I have, and focus on the important issues facing our nation and the world."[3] While many were outraged at the content of the tapes, others wrote it off as locker-room talk or the kind of things guys talk about when no one else is listening. These events supported the "boys will be boys" mentality.

The common phrase "boys will be boys" is also used to excuse negative behavior, as if boys and men should not be held accountable for poor choices and bad judgment. Elizabeth J. Meyer, PhD, a writer for *Psychology Today*, says, "The expression 'boys will be boys' attempts to explain away aggressive behaviors that a small number of children exhibit by linking it with 'natural' or 'biological' impulses, without examining other reasons for the aggression."[4] Instead of the behavior being corrected, it is reinforced and rewarded, written off because the person was born male.

Although girls and women are more outspoken in modern America compared with decades ago, this is a relatively new behavior. The women's rights movements in the early 1900s and the feminist movements that began in the 1960s gave women the courage to speak their minds and voice their concerns, despite the backlash and ridicule they received from men and other women who were content with women's status in society.

Today, feminists speak out for women's rights to behave as they wish without facing assaults on their gender. They also fight for equality of all genders. But the term *feminist* has received a negative connotation, associated with hating men. As an extreme example of how people feel toward feminists, Pat Robertson, a popular televised Christian minister, stated that the feminist agenda is "a socialist, anti-family political movement that encourages women to leave their husbands, kill their children, practice witchcraft, destroy capitalism and become lesbians."[5]

SPORTS ARE FOR MEN

Despite the increased number of women athletes and overall participation in sports, coverage for women's sports has decreased in the past decades. Los Angeles sports networks devoted 5 percent of their airtime to women's sports in 1989. In 2014, such airtime was down to 3.2 percent.[6]

It's not just the amount of airtime that sets male and female professional athletes apart. Even off the court or field, athletes are treated differently based on their gender. In the article "He's a Laker; She's a 'Looker': The

THE ROLE OF FEMINISM

The feminist movements from the 1960s to the present have given women voices to demand the same opportunities that are given to men. It wasn't until the 1970s that women could get a credit card without the written approval of a husband or father. Betty Friedan, author of *The Feminine Mystique*, published her book in 1963 to make readers think about why society encourages women to continue in the basic lifestyle of parent and homemaker and discourages them from looking for fulfillment outside of the home through careers and social organizations. Feminism has played a positive role in helping women make progress in legal and social areas, but there is still a division between today's feminists. Some radical feminist ideas attempt to dismantle the traditional family structure, which many women, feminist or not, believe is an important part of a fulfilling and happy life.

Having open and honest conversations about the differences between male and female experiences in America can help people understand various perspectives.

Consequences of Gender-Stereotypical Portrayals of Male and Female Athletes by the Print Media," authors Jennifer Knight and Traci Giuliano say, "Sport commentators and writers often allude or explicitly refer to a female athlete's attractiveness, emotionality, femininity, and heterosexuality (all of which effectively convey to the audience that her stereotypical gender role is more salient than her athletic role)." Knight and Giuliano go on to state that male athletes are shown by the media as "powerful, independent, dominating, and valued."[7] Male athletes do not ask reporters for this type of treatment.

But reporters and sports viewers place female athletes in a position that disregards their athletic ability. This is an example of a privilege that female athletes lack, a privilege of being taken seriously that their male counterparts achieve naturally.

OBJECTIFYING ADVERTISEMENTS

Women's bodies are also frequently put on display in advertising for print and online media, which are less likely to objectify men. Often, advertising that targets men portrays women as objects. The only time advertisements exclude men as targets is when the products are assumed to be exclusively for women, such as feminine hygiene products, household cleaners, and products for children. A few brands have broken the stereotype, such as Diet Coke, which attempted to sell soft drinks to women by showing a man quenching his thirst with his shirt off.

A 2015 advertising campaign for Carl's Jr. burgers caused

IGNORING WOMEN'S SPORTS

Topics covered by sports networks instead of women's sports as noted by USC News included a swarm of bees invading a Red Sox vs. Yankees professional baseball game; an 18-inch corn dog at the Arizona Diamondbacks' baseball stadium; former Dodgers manager Tommy Lasorda's new restaurant opening; whether professional basketball player Kendall Marshall will be able to find a decent burrito when he goes to Milwaukee; and a stray dog who has become beloved by fans at the Milwaukee Brewers' baseball stadium.

many people to object to the sexualization of the woman in the ad. The commercial led with a barely dressed blonde strolling down a street full of men, who ogled at her with dropped jaws. Specially angled camera shots hid the woman's bathing suit top and short-shorts, leading the viewer to believe she was completely naked. There were shots of watermelons covering her breasts and an apple covering her bottom when she was viewed from the back. About 20 seconds into the commercial, the viewer gets a full-frontal shot of the bikini-clad woman biting into a juicy burger as the men continue to stare.

The advertisement targeted men and capitalized on the sexualization of women. The thought behind the commercial is that men like girls in bikinis, so they'll also like the burger. Other than selling a burger, this ad also normalizes the notion that women are sex objects. In 2017, Carl's Jr. changed its ads to appeal to more consumers. The company released a new ad that made fun of how it had sexualized women to sell burgers.

The sexualized portrayal of women in the media sends a strong message that the value of a woman rests solely in her body. According to Shadia Duske, a psychotherapist and the founder of Luna Counseling Center, "Audiences are more likely to be persuaded to buy a product if the advertising narrative is easily recognizable and frequently repeated." Duske also says, "But if these ads represent what is easily recognizable and 'normal,' what does that say about the health of our society?"[8]

DISCUSSION STARTERS

- Why do companies attempt to sell their products by putting them next to nearly nude women? Why do you think this sexual representation of women helps products sell?

- Why does American society allow boys to get a free pass for negative behavior? Should all children be subject to the same behavioral expectations regardless of gender? Explain your reasoning.

- What are some examples of women in television or film playing a leading role in which they are represented in a powerful position or hold a prominent position in a professional career?

- With so many female athletes and high-quality female sports today, why do you believe there is a lack of coverage and attention?

CHAPTER THREE

FREE
SPEECH

The First Amendment in the US Constitution includes the right to free speech. However, men are encouraged to practice this right more than women. Men are able to dominate conversations without others viewing them as loudmouths or too talkative. They can interrupt people to ensure their opinions are heard without facing as many negative reactions as a woman would. And when men talk, people generally assume they know what they are talking about. Additionally, it is an acceptable practice for a man to question the validity of a woman's knowledge and to explain to her why he knows more than she does. These examples support the invisible privilege men have in everyday conversations.

INTERRUPTIONS

Society has trained people to believe that male opinions are more important than women's and that men can take over conversations when they see fit. Women are more likely to be interrupted by both men and women when they talk. Interruptions happen in social settings, at home, and in the workplace. There is even evidence that female Supreme Court justices get cut off more frequently than male justices when they speak.

A 2017 study by Tonja Jacobi and Dylan Schweers from Northwestern University Pritzker School of Law reviewed transcripts of Supreme Court hearings. The findings were presented in their paper, "Justice, Interrupted: The Effect of Gender, Ideology and Seniority at Supreme Court Oral Arguments." In 2017, the Supreme Court was made up of six men and three women. The study reviewed records from 1990, 2002, and 2015, and from public records of Chief Justice John Roberts's oral arguments. Results showed that the female justices were interrupted much more than males by other Supreme Court justices and lawyers.

THE IMPACT OF CONSTRAINING OPINIONS

Interrupting women can simply appear to be bad manners, but the effects can be damaging. Consider the interruption of the Supreme Court justices. As more women have joined the Supreme Court, interruptions have significantly increased. When the female justices' questions aren't answered and their statements are cut off midway through, their voices are not fully being considered in the outcome of the hearings. By eliminating the female contribution to the debates, the Supreme Court decisions are being skewed in favor of the male-dominated bench. In general, since the first woman joined the bench, the female justices have been more liberal and the male justices more conservative. Supreme Court verdicts may end up being more conservative overall.

Justice Ruth Bader Ginsburg was interrupted six times more than male justices. Justice Sonia Sotomayor was interrupted three times as much as male justices.

Because of societal norms, it is often acceptable or expected for men to dominate conversations.

And Justice Elena Kagan was interrupted more than twice the amount the male justices were.[1] Roberts and Justice Samuel Alito are the male counterparts in the study. There is a rule against interrupting justices, but Roberts does not always enforce it.

DOMINANCE IN CONVERSATIONS

Another instance of male privilege is the ability to dominate conversations without judgment. Women are frequently regarded as too talkative when they speak up. But numerous studies show men are more likely to dominate conversations, meaning that men talk more than women in most public and formal settings.

Two Canadian researchers compared 63 studies that evaluated the amount of time American men and women spoke in different situations. Out of the 63 studies, women dominated the conversation only twice.[2] Studies in other countries came to similar conclusions, finding that men more frequently dominate conversations. The amount of time a woman spends talking increases in social settings with mostly other women, like at friends' houses or at gatherings in bars and restaurants. But in mixed groups with both men and women, men still tend to dominate the conversation.

Although evidence shows that men talk more, this behavior is perceived as acceptable. Women who attempt to increase their amount of time talking are often considered pesky or annoying.

YOU TALK TOO MUCH

Talking in class, whether answering questions or offering opposing viewpoints in discussions, can be perceived as showing off. Girls are more likely than boys to choose not to speak rather than face criticism from other students. A male science teacher tried to encourage equal participation from girls and boys. He noticed that even though talk time was about equal between girls and boys, the boys complained the girls were getting too much time and attention.

DO YOU KNOW WHAT YOU'RE TALKING ABOUT?

It's an assumption in American society that when men speak, they know what they are talking about. They can

WOMEN ALSO KNOW STUFF

Women Also Know Stuff is a website created to promote female scholars in political science. Men are called on as experts to be speakers and representatives for a variety of reasons, while equally qualified women are often overlooked. Women Also Know Stuff offers a database of female scholars that academics and journalists can turn to for information on a wealth of subjects so that female experts can also share their knowledge with others.

give directions and provide up-to-date information on subjects ranging from life to politics to local news. They are presumed intelligent until proven otherwise. But it's more difficult for women to be thought of this way. People have the habit of automatically questioning a woman's intelligence. Even when a woman knows what she is talking about, men will often challenge her knowledge and talk down to her, even if they have incomplete knowledge on the topic. This incorrect assumption that the man knows more about the topic than the woman he is speaking with is known as *mansplaining*.

Online news and lifestyle website the *Observer* featured an article about mansplaining stories that women shared on Twitter. A women's studies student asked others to share the worst things they've had mansplained to them, and the response was overwhelming. Women reported that men have explained everything from breastfeeding to how to spell names properly. One

Rebecca Solnit has written books on feminism and social change.

woman's coworker told her that she misspelled her own name. Another man tried to explain to a librarian the proper way to search for a book by its title and author. Another instance of mansplaining occurred when a male paramedic explained to a woman that giving birth was only about as painful or difficult as defecating.

Before *mansplaining* became a mainstream term, author Rebecca Solnit wrote an article called *Men Explain Things to Me*. She explains how some men explain things to women with confidence and arrogance, whether they know what they are talking about or not. Solnit believes these men feel the need to put women in a lower place on the totem pole by out-talking them with imaginary knowledge. Solnit goes on to point out that constant mansplaining takes a personal toll on women because "it trains us in self-doubt and self-limitation just as it exercises men's unsupported overconfidence."[3]

Men may not even realize these interactions are belittling to women. They may truly believe they are more familiar with a topic than the woman they are speaking with. In many cases, this is due to the upbringing they received. In US society they have learned to assume their knowledge is greater than a woman's and is perceived as more valuable.

CONSTANT APOLOGIZING

In everyday conversations, women are constantly asking for pardons for mundane acts. A shampoo commercial once asked, why are women always apologizing? The ad showed circumstances with women apologizing, as one woman apologized for asking a colleague a question and another apologized to someone who took her chair.

Male privilege in these situations is apparent when men can come into a room, take up space, and expect to participate in conversations without apologizing for it. This privilege is not necessarily asked for, but it is given to most men and boys nonetheless.

Women apologize to be polite and to show others that they are not trying to be overpowering. Women were once expected to be quiet and submissive, but in modern America they play a significant role in work, religion, politics, and the social realm. Women's ingrained need to apologize for participating in these activities is an instance of their lack of privilege.

While the right to free speech was intended to apply to all citizens, women's freedom of speech is often silenced and undermined by the male privilege that leads society to believe male voices are more entitled to be heard than female ones.

DISCUSSION STARTERS

- Do you think society puts more value on what a man says than what a woman says? Explain your reasoning.
- Interrupting a woman on the Supreme Court is allowed by her male colleagues. Why do you believe this is?
- Do you believe women are silenced and criticized for speaking their opinions? Why or why not?

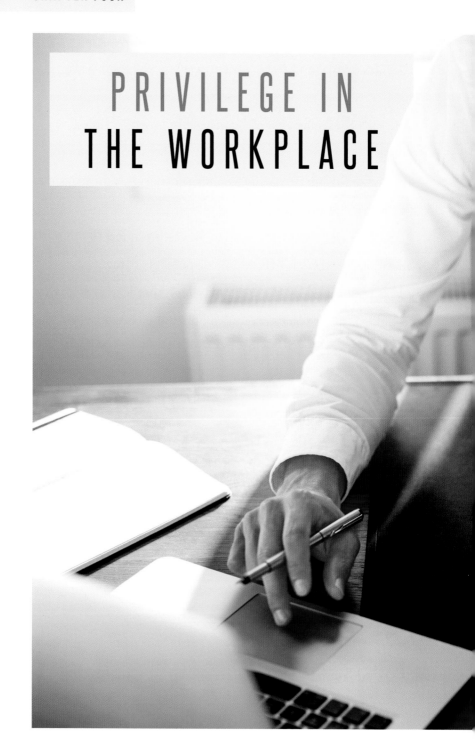

CHAPTER FOUR

PRIVILEGE IN
THE WORKPLACE

Easily identifiable instances of male privilege can be seen in the workplace. Discrimination and harassment against women in the workplace have plagued the United States for decades. But the easiest way to identify male privilege on the job is by noting the amount of harassment women face compared to men and considering the paychecks of men and women.

The Civil Rights Act of 1964 forbids discrimination based on sex, but women continue to be affected by less pay for equal work. In 1961, President John F. Kennedy established the Commission on the Status of Women to investigate equality for women at work, in education, and under the law. After investigating women's circumstances, significant instances of workplace discrimination were discovered. The recommendations from the report aimed at reducing workplace discrimination against women, and included paid maternity leave, wage improvements, and affordable

RACIAL INEQUALITIES

When Kennedy's Commission on the Status of Women was looking for ways to support women in the workplace, African-American female advisers made suggestions that indicated needs for women of color that were different from the needs of white women. The Equal Pay Act of 1963 prohibited discrimination based on race, but recommendations regarding minorities were left out of the final report.

childcare. The Equal Pay Act of 1963 was created based on the report. It prohibits employers from paying some people less than others because of their gender, race, or religion.

Although progress has been made to decrease gender-based discrimination toward women in the workplace, women continue to encounter difficulties. Women experience a significant wage gap compared with men, earning approximately 72 cents for every dollar a man makes.[1] In addition, many companies don't offer paid maternity leave to mothers. This situation can pressure women into returning to work quickly after giving birth.

WORKPLACE HARASSMENT

Another instance of privilege in the workplace stems from men's smaller chance of experiencing sexual harassment. The Equal Employment Opportunity Commission tracks charges of sexual harassment in the workplace. In the complaints received between 2010 and 2016, most victims were women. Sexual harassment claims by men accounted for approximately 17 percent.[2] Sexual harassment can take many forms, from jokes and gestures to direct touching and unwanted advances.

Men who harass women in the workplace often threaten to retaliate if a woman reports the inappropriate behavior. The perpetrator can make work miserable for the woman and can sometimes cause her to lose her job. A recent survey claims 32 percent of women polled had experienced sexual harassment, and 70 percent of those women did not report it.[3] Some expressed fear of retaliation as their reason for not reporting the harassment. Women who have children to care for or are the primary breadwinners for their family are especially unlikely to report harassment out of fear that they might lose their job and steady source of income.

Additionally, female victims are sometimes punished when they attempt to address the inappropriate behavior of men. An example of this occurred when Susan Fowler, a former engineer at a transport company called Uber, reported an instance of sexual harassment. Her manager messaged her over company chat and implied that he would like to have sexual relations with her.

SILENCED BY POWER

Even prominent people in esteemed careers are not free from discrimination and sexual harassment. In 2017, American film producer Harvey Weinstein was accused of sexual assault and harassment by dozens of female actresses and models. Weinstein is known as one of the most powerful producers in Hollywood, and women have stated that he used his influence and power to lure them into uncomfortable situations and keep them from talking about it. Actors such as Gwyneth Paltrow and Angelina Jolie have come forward saying Weinstein invited them to his hotel room for business meetings and made unwanted sexual advances.

Harassment creates a hostile work environment.

Fowler documented the messages and reported him to the company's human resources (HR) department. She was told by HR and upper management that while this instance was a clear case of sexual harassment, they were not going to fire her manager. Instead, they told Fowler that she could leave her job. They also told Fowler if she stayed, she would likely receive a poor performance review by her manager because of her report.

THE WAGE GAP

The difference in pay between men and women is the most common example of privilege in the workplace, and the wage gap is larger for women of color. African-American women earned only 63 percent of a white man's full-time salary, and Hispanic women earned only 54 percent. Asian women have the smallest wage gap, earning 85 percent of a white man's salary.[4]

The wage gap varies from state to state and between industries, but men almost always have the bigger paychecks. Wyoming has the largest wage gap, where men's average earnings are 29 percent more than women's. California males earn 25 percent more.[5] Rhode Island, Connecticut, and the District of Columbia are great states for working women who desire equal pay, since women average higher earnings than men for the same job in these states.

Industries such as administrative services, the arts, and food services have smaller wage gaps between men and women. However, more prestigious industries such as technology, science, public administration, and finance have much larger differences between the earnings of men and women. Finance and insurance have the widest gap, with men averaging 29 percent more than women.[6]

In 1963, the Equal Pay Act was passed to ensure that employers could not pay women less based on their gender. Back then, women only earned 59 percent of a man's salary.[7] The wage gap has slowly narrowed, and other cases have clarified wage discrimination. In 1970, the *Schultz v. Wheaton Glass Company* case ruled that job titles cannot be changed to pay a woman less than a man.

The wage gap has long-term effects on women. Making less money throughout their careers means women have less money to save or invest. Therefore, they have fewer resources to live on when they retire.

According to the Department of Labor, as of 2015, 57 percent of all women participate in the US workforce, and that number is rising.[8] With so many women in the workforce, equal pay for equal work continues to be a frequently debated topic.

EQUAL WORK, UNEQUAL PAY

Lilly Ledbetter was a Goodyear employee for 19 years. She was anonymously notified that she was receiving thousands of dollars less than male employees who held similar management positions. Ledbetter filed a discrimination case and a jury awarded her $3 million.[9] The case was appealed and sent to the Supreme Court, which voted in favor of Goodyear. The court based its decision on a law that says the difference in pay must be reported within 180 days of the first paycheck. Lilly continued to fight for equal pay, and in 2009 the Lilly Ledbetter Fair Pay Restoration Act was signed by President Barack Obama. The new law states that the discrepancy must be reported within 180 days of the last unequal paycheck.

POSITIONS OF POWER

Even women who hold high positions of power within a company are underrepresented and underpaid. When Bloomberg released the list of highest-paid CEOs of 2016, only a small percentage were women. And only one woman made it to the top 10: Ginni Rometty, the CEO of IBM.

Overall, fewer women hold high-level positions. Of 346 executives of Fortune 500 companies, only 21 were women. For every 100 women who are promoted to management, 130 men are pushed up the same ladder.[10]

The bias starts early on in women's careers. Women who ask for promotions are viewed as less likable because they are too pushy. But men who seek out promotions are given them because they are viewed as go-getters.

Starting from a young age, men have the privilege of being

DAUGHTERS AT WORK

Take Your Daughter to Work Day began in 1992. New discussions were happening about women in the workplace, especially surrounding the subjects of job harassment and higher pay for women. The Ms. Foundation came up with the idea that parents should bring their daughters to work so girls could see what opportunities are available, explore what they might be interested in, and ask questions. Feminist Gloria Steinem explained the concept to *Parade* magazine, and Take Your Daughter to Work Day went full force. This was an important step in helping girls see more women in the workplace and giving them the encouragement to pursue careers they might have thought were unavailable to them.

taught that they can have successful, powerful positions that will provide them with the financial means to live a prosperous life. Boys see these male role models on television and in films, on the local news, in advertising campaigns, and by way of real-life examples of friends and family members. Girls have limited examples of successful women in powerful positions, and the media frequently teaches women to use their bodies to entertain others.

DIFFERENCES IN CAREER

Certain careers are labeled pink-collar jobs, which are filled predominantly by women. These jobs include nurses, teachers, human resources managers, and public relations professionals. And while these specific examples are well-paying, reliable sources of income, other pink-collar jobs don't share the same benefits.

The food service industry, housekeeping, childcare, and in-home care aides are all areas filled with predominantly female workers. But they are low-paying and unreliable sources of income. A restaurant server may earn $100 in tips one night and $22 the next; there is no steady income guarantee. The 2010 edition of *Women in American Society* shows that in 2007, 592,000 women were food servers, compared with the 274,000 men holding these positions. Women earned an average of

In many states, waiters and waitresses don't get paid minimum wage. They rely on tips for a large portion of their income.

$360 per week, while the men brought home an average of $415. The same publication lists data for maids and housekeepers, with 717,000 female workers and 132,000 male employees. Women averaged $357 per week, but the men earned $439.[11]

Beginning at a young age, girls are typically socialized to lean toward traditionally female careers. They are encouraged to play with dolls or to maintain an imaginary house, and they are praised when they act nurturing.

Working women with children face additional issues with the wage gap. If women leave their careers for a period of time to take care of their children, some of them face difficulties in finding new jobs later on. Women who do rejoin the workforce find that on average their annual income has decreased by approximately one-third of what it used to be.[12]

Male privilege is identifiable in many areas of the workplace, from paychecks to the amount of harassment women undergo compared with men. One of the biggest challenges to overcome is showing girls that women can also be successful in various professions so that when they grow up, more girls will attempt to break into roles that have been traditionally assigned to men, such as CEOs, head chefs, and executive directors.

DISCUSSION STARTERS

- Despite efforts to improve equality for women in the workplace, what barriers are preventing women from achieving the same successes as men?
- What environmental factors enable some men to get away with sexual harassment?
- What factors contribute to lower earnings for women?

CHAPTER FIVE

FAMILY AND RELATIONSHIPS

In traditional family structures with a mother, father, and children, men often take on fewer responsibilities around the house. Men typically get a free pass when it comes to household chores and taking care of the kids. Until the mid-twentieth century, society assumed middle- and upper-class men were primary income earners and women stayed home. The household chores and taking care of the kids naturally fell to the mothers. This typically held true even in families where the mother worked outside the home.

MORE WORK FOR WOMEN

A study from the University of Michigan shows that having a husband creates an extra seven hours of housework per week for women.[3] Husbands perform outside chores like mowing and gardening, but having a wife still reduces men's general housework time by an hour each week.

Still, today, even with more than 50 percent of women working outside of the home, many home and childcare tasks are still the mother's responsibility.[1] Studies show that even mothers who are the primary breadwinners of the family still carry the heavier workload at home. In 2013, the Bureau of Labor Statistics found that women spent 2 hours and 13 minutes a day on chores. Men clocked in at 1 hour and 21 minutes.[2]

WOMEN'S BIOLOGICAL CLOCKS

So, when are you going to have kids? It's a common question that women frequently get from family and friends once they reach their 20s and 30s. Men less commonly have to answer this seemingly innocent, yet extremely personal, question.

There's a notion in American society that men don't necessarily need to have children to lead fulfilling lives. Men can choose to have children or not, without being judged negatively by their peers. Men who decide not to have children because they don't want the responsibility or because they don't think they would be good parents are praised for having enough foresight to make this decision.

On the other hand, women who choose not to have children are commonly viewed in a more negative light. They are seen as selfish and irresponsible. Society has pushed the belief that a woman will never be fulfilled if she doesn't have kids and that she will regret her decision.

SETTING THE STAGE

In May 1955, *Good Housekeeping* magazine published an article about how to be a good housewife. It advised that women let their husbands speak first when arriving home from work, as their topics of conversation were more important. Women were told not to complain if their husbands were late for dinner or didn't bother coming home, because they probably had a difficult day. It told women not to question their husbands' judgment or actions because the men were the masters of the house and women had no right to question them.

Because of this belief, many people believe having children should be a woman's natural goal. Women are encouraged to hurry up and have kids. They are constantly reminded that their biological clocks are ticking.

WORKING PARENTS

Men are not subjected to the same level of judgment and criticism that women face when it comes to parenting and lifestyle choices. When a man has both a career and children, he is not typically treated as if he is being a neglectful parent.

In American society, the married man is assumed to be the breadwinner, or the main income earner of the family, because men have historically earned more than women. Men are encouraged and expected to pursue careers. When children are born, it is typically the father who goes back to work while the mother is expected to stay home to care for the children. The roots for this family model

Some families can barely afford the high expenses of childcare, even with two incomes.

reach back decades, when the white woman's traditional role was at home, raising children.

Minorities faced different struggles through the 1900s, and many African-American and Hispanic women had to work outside the home to support their families, often at low-paying jobs. Now, many women, white and minority alike, hold full-time jobs. The Department of Labor reports that 70 percent of women with children under age 18 are working.[4] And childcare is expensive. According to

MAIDEN NAMES

In 2011, a man followed the instructions he was given by the DMV to officially change his last name to his wife's after they married, instead of having her take his name. A year later, he was told that his license was suspended because his name change was considered fraud. Men, they said, can't change their names like women can without a court order. After a court appeal with his lawyer and official documentation of his name change, the DMV reinstated his license. At that time, only nine states allowed men to take their wives' last names, but not many men had ever really tried. This is one instance of the deeply embedded cultural norms that separate women and men from true equality.

BabyCenter, a popular website for new parents, the average cost of childcare per month is approximately $1,000.[5]

In most families today, both parents are employed. Hilary Rosen, a communications and political consultant and expert, wrote, "I admire women who can stay home and raise their kids full-time. . . . It is a wonderful luxury to have the choice. But let's stipulate that it is NOT a choice that most women have in America today."[6] The cost of living has increased significantly over the past decades. The Economic Policy Institute reported that earnings for middle-wage employees have only increased by 6 percent since 1979. Productivity has increased by more than 70 percent.[7] Americans are producing more goods and providing more services, but their wages are not improving, and the cost for goods and services is continuing to rise. Because of the economic and financial situation of most families, many women can no longer afford to stay home.

BABYSITTING THE KIDS

Society expects that mothers should be primary caregivers. Many men receive praise for performing regular parenting duties such as bathing their kids and caring for them when the mother is away from the home. Mothers, on the other hand, are expected to perform the same tasks while being subject to various levels of judgment about how well they are performing.

When women are away from their children, people ask who is with their kids. If the children's father is watching them, it's not uncommon for the father's actions to be referred to as babysitting. This simple comment shows a divide in what many people expect from mothers versus fathers.

Mothers are not referred to as babysitters when they take care of their children; it's a role women are expected to undertake. Society allows men to slide by as secondary caretakers. Performing basic childcare functions such as feeding and playing with their children is regarded as noteworthy or special instead of ordinary and expected.

Best-selling author Adam Mansbach says, "I get undue adulation all of the time for simply being out with my kid;

Kids benefit when both parents contribute equally to raising them.

just because my kid isn't freezing to death, I'm a great father." He has written about the struggle parents go through to get their kids to sleep every night, but even he admits he's only involved in the bedtime battle 25 percent of the time. The other 75 percent falls on his wife.[8]

In general, men are required to do very little to be viewed as good parents. They have the benefit of receiving words of commendation and approval, while women are under constant observation and are critiqued for their parenting. Meanwhile, in other areas of family and relationships, mothers are putting in more work with full-time jobs, acting as primary caregivers, and taking on the bulk of the household chores. Men still benefit from the old patriarchal views that they should go to work while women take care of the children and home.

DISCUSSION STARTERS

- Why do you think men receive more positive reinforcement than women for performing basic childcare tasks?
- How would you divide up a family's household chores to create a more equal division of labor?
- Families with two working parents are common today. How do you think this has changed family values and expectations for men and women in the home?

CHAPTER SIX

HEALTH AND
BODY IMAGE

Women face a disproportionate amount of criticism regarding appearance and body type compared with men. Moreover, medical testing and research focus more commonly on symptoms that men experience and on developing treatments for those symptoms. Meanwhile, women and their different symptoms are sometimes ignored and overlooked.

LOSING WEIGHT

The weight loss industry generates more than $55 billion in revenue each year. In 2007, 10.6 million women received a surgical or nonsurgical cosmetic procedure.[1] The top five cosmetic procedures for women were breast augmentation, liposuction, eyelid surgery, abdominoplasty, and breast reduction. There was also a trend of parents giving their high school graduates breast implants as gifts. From 2002 to 2003, the number of 18-year-olds undergoing surgery tripled.

Women's bodies are constantly critiqued, but it's impossible for almost everyone to reach the ideal standard of beauty set in America. Women are labeled as too fat if they don't have the same measurements as the models in fashion magazines. But on the contrary, if a woman is thin, many assume she has an eating disorder. Even though both boys and girls report being concerned about their weight as early as elementary school, men are much less likely to be judged or shamed for their weight and appearance. While girls and women often struggle with body dysmorphia, a belief that one's body is flawed that leads to an obsession with hiding it or trying to fix it, boys have a different struggle. Boys and men are now showing signs of muscle dysmorphia, believing that they are not masculine enough or that there is something wrong with their bodies if they do not have the same muscular appearance as the men featured in the media.

The Body Project was created by Bradley University in Illinois to study how body image impacts both men and women. The project notes that men are much quieter about voicing their dissatisfaction with their bodies. However, research has found that while both men and women suffer from negative consequences related to body image, women are affected more than men.

BODY IMAGE

With the media focusing on the importance of weight and appearance, both girls and boys are struggling with how they look. Most of the criticism falls on women and girls, so the percentage of boys and men who are affected is generally lower. A survey of teens in grades 9 through 12 revealed more than 59 percent of the girls and 29 percent of the boys were trying to lose weight to improve how their bodies looked based on the standard of beauty that is represented in today's media. The ideal size of women, as portrayed by models, is 13 to 19 percent below the normal, healthy weight. In a study of more than 3,000 women, 89 percent wanted to lose weight.[2]

High school students who consumed hours of mainstream media were asked to rate the importance of women's qualities. They attributed greater importance to sexiness and beauty than the students who spent less time consuming mainstream media.

A woman can spend thousands of dollars on makeup over her lifetime.

The rate of depression in girls and women doubled between 2000 and 2010, according to the documentary *Miss Representation* by Jennifer Siebel Newsom. This dramatic increase is attributed to the increasing pressure on females to have the right body type, wear the right clothes, and look like the women in the media and on the pages of fashion magazines. There is a constant negativity toward women in the media about their weight and how they look. Today, the majority of images of women are digitally enhanced so the results shown on the pages of magazines and in scenes from movies are impossible to achieve naturally. This level of beauty is unattainable and causes girls and women to feel as if they aren't good enough because they don't look like the digitally altered models and actresses. *Miss Representation* reports that 53 percent of 13-year-old girls are unhappy with their bodies. The film also claims that 65 percent of women and girls have an eating disorder in some form.[3]

THE PRICE OF BEING A WOMAN

Male grooming and hygiene is simple and relatively inexpensive. If a man gets his hair cut, maintains his facial hair, and brushes his teeth, he's considered clean-cut and well-groomed, and his daily hygiene routine is minimal. Women, on the other hand, are expected to dye and style their hair and apply makeup daily (and keep it fresh throughout the day) to make themselves more presentable in public.

Even skin and hair care products that are similar are priced lower when they are targeted to men. *Business Insider* did a study in 2015 and compared a few items that were the same but targeted to men versus women. It found that the Schick Hydro razor had a women's price point of $9.97, and for men it was $8.56. It also found that Neutrogena Anti-Wrinkle Cream cost $11.42 for women and $10.35 for men.[4]

During the same year, a different comparison shopper for *Cosmopolitan* magazine found that Dove shampoo cost $4.99 for women, but the same product targeted toward men cost only $3.99. Neutrogena face wash was $10.49 for women, but when labeled for men it cost only $8.49. And Degree deodorant for women rang up at $3.89. The same version for men was only $2.49.[5] The basic act of shopping shows male privilege in the aisles of department stores.

According to *Miss Representation*, the media and advertising industries show women and girls that their path to power or success lies in how good men think they look and how pretty they are. Other news sources report that the average woman in the United States spends $15,000 on beauty products in her lifetime.[6]

CLOTHING SENDS A MESSAGE

Men can wear relaxed, comfortable clothing day after day, while women are expected to wear new, stylish outfits. And just like beauty products and services, women's clothes are also generally more expensive than men's.

Women are labeled for how they dress or don't dress. They can be called trashy or slutty for wearing a tank top with a bra strap showing or wearing short skirts or shorts. Women can also be labeled as prudish or unfashionable if they dress too conservatively. Many people argue that women should be

REVEALING COSTUMES

Halloween is a holiday when the sexualization of women's bodies is apparent. The costumes targeted to girls and women range from Disney princesses to superheroes to workplace professionals. And these costumes all have something in common: they are shrunken in size to sexualize the character and show as much skin as possible. But the men's shelves aren't stocked with costumes meant to objectify their bodies. This is another example of how women's clothing is designed to catch the attention of people around them.

Journalist Katie Couric's appearance, such as her clothes and makeup, was frequently critiqued while she served as an anchorwoman.

allowed to wear what they want without facing judgment from others.

Most male clothing departments include a variety of shirts, shorts, and pants. Female clothing departments have a sea of shirts, tank tops, pants, shorts, skirts, dresses, and accessories. Men's clothing is made to be roomy and comfortable, while many styles for girls and women are body-hugging and revealing. One mother, Stephanie Giese, voiced her concern in a blog post that went viral when she called out retailer Target for the short shorts and tight-fitting clothing that flooded the shelves of the girls' section. She also went to Kohl's department store and photographed the boys' and girls' clothing sold there. The girls' clothing bared significantly more skin than the boys' clothing.

SEEKING MEDICAL HELP

Evidence shows that people, including doctors and other medical staff, perceive women's pain as exaggerated or fabricated. Some studies, such as "The Girl Who Cried Pain," show that women are treated less aggressively for their symptoms and are often misdiagnosed.

Medical care tends to be quicker and more effective for men. The nationwide average for men to wait for care when experiencing abdominal pain is 49 minutes.

PAYING FOR MEDICAL CARE

Before President Obama implemented the Affordable Care Act (ACA) in 2010, women were paying $1 billion more for their health insurance premiums than men.[9] Even though the ACA banned gender-based premiums, women can still expect to pay approximately 13 percent more for long-term health insurance premiums because they are expected to live longer.[10] Only 12 percent of individual health insurance plans in the United States covered maternity care before the ACA.[11] When the ACA went into effect, it required insurance companies to provide coverage for critical women's health services such as maternity care, prescription drug coverage, and mental health care. A common male complaint about the ACA is that it is required to include coverage for maternity care, and some men don't want to pay for a service they say doesn't apply to them.

The average wait for women is 65 minutes.[7]

For years, clinical trials and drug research only included male patients. So, the treatment for medical conditions and the medicines being used to combat diseases were designed based on the symptoms and responses of male patients. Because of the lack of research on women, drug companies and doctors are treating women with the same drugs even though treatments may affect males and females differently.

Heart disease is the number one cause of death for American men and women, and women have different causes and symptoms than men. But heart disease research has also been largely focused on men, with women making up only one-third of the clinical trial patients and with only 31 percent of the trials' results including gender.[8]

In the mental health and medical fields, women face different struggles than men. They may need to work harder than men to convince doctors they need medical care and that they are not just being overly sensitive or hysterical. In addition, while men and boys also have struggles with weight and body issues, society places a stronger emphasis on the beauty of women and girls. The female body bears the bulk of the criticism and demand to appeal to others, generally men. Because of this pressure, women and girls are struggling physically, mentally, and emotionally.

DISCUSSION STARTERS

- How can people ensure that women receive the same health care benefits as men?
- In what ways are women devalued by people who place more emphasis on body type and appearance than on personality and intelligence?
- Is it the government's responsibility to ensure quality health care for women? Explain your reasoning.

CHAPTER SEVEN

PRIVILEGE IN EDUCATION

The education system is biased in favor of the male gender in various ways. Dress codes determine what girls can and can't wear, emphasizing that items like leggings and tank tops are inappropriate and distract boys from learning. The history curriculum is heavily weighted with information about the accomplishments of white men. In addition, teachers tend to pay more attention to male students than to female students.

DRESS CODES

School dress codes have been in place for years. Girls historically have been sent home more frequently than boys for problems with the dress code. In the 1960s and early 1970s, girls were not permitted to wear pants to school. They had to wear dresses or skirts, and school administrators frequently checked their length. They made girls kneel in the hallways. If the girls' skirts or dresses didn't touch the floor as they knelt, they violated the dress code.

Today, it's not uncommon for girls to be removed from class and asked to cover up or leave because their attire goes against policy rules. Often, school administrators will say that the students were sent home because their outfits were distracting to boys. Many schools have

Young girls who wear tank tops to school have been sent home because the dress code says they are revealing too much skin.

banned leggings, yoga pants, skinny jeans, and other tight-fitting bottoms because they believe the clothing too closely defines girls' bodies.

Schools are consistently sending the message that it's the boys' privilege to learn without distraction, while many girls are sent home because of their appearance and are forced to miss out on learning time. This also sends the message that boys don't need to learn to control themselves and their thoughts about girls. Instead, dress codes send the message that girls are supposed to remain covered to prevent boys from having inappropriate or distracting thoughts.

PRIVILEGE IN EDUCATION

The curricula used in schools from kindergarten through high school teach students about the contributions white men have made to history and the world. Girls and women, on the other hand, are highly underrepresented in school curricula. Because of this, girls do not learn about many would-be female role models from history.

This system has been the method of education for decades. Studies from the 1960s, 1970s, and 1980s showed that women were practically nonexistent in schoolbooks, with only 3 percent of the books highlighting women. A more recent study reviewed 18 high school books for American history classes. These textbooks featured 12,382 men or boys and 1,335 women or girls. In addition, there were 616 illustrations that featured women and 3,505 illustrations that featured men.[1] While the ratio of women to men and the overall number of women included has increased, there continues to be a shortage of women in history books.

Gender stereotypes also negatively affect girls and their education. One of the most prominent stereotypes is that men and boys are superior in math and science. And despite the trend of developing science, technology, engineering, and math (STEM) programs to encourage more female involvement in these areas, the gender bias still exists.

A study in 2012 assigned fake names to male and female applicants to a university science program. Both male and female faculty rated the male applicants as more competent and hirable than female applicants with identical application materials. In 2014, a study found that male and female hiring managers were more likely to hire a man for a job requiring math skills.

Women in math- and science-related fields report their success is often questioned and they are asked to prove themselves repeatedly. Sixty-three percent of white women have been asked to provide additional evidence to prove their competence both in interviews and on the job. That number jumps to 77 percent for African-American women.[2]

UNDERREPRESENTATION IN TEXTBOOKS

Author and researcher Rebecca Alber reviewed school curriculum materials being used in 2016 in the Los Angeles Unified School District (LAUSD). LAUSD is the second-largest school district in the United States, and 52 percent of the district population is female. Alber reviewed language arts textbooks for grades eight, nine, and ten. In the eighth-grade textbooks, less than 30 percent of the authors of text excerpts used in teaching were female, with the other two grades showing similar results. The publisher of the textbooks is one of the largest textbook publishers in the United States. Its textbooks are found in most classrooms across the nation. That means the majority of students in the United States are exposed to women authors in textbooks less than one-third of the time.[3]

LIKE A GIRL

In 2014, the feminine product company Always made a commercial called "Like a Girl." Participants were asked to describe what it meant to run like a girl, throw like a girl, and fight like a girl. Older male and female participants first displayed stereotypical girl-like actions. They flailed their limbs around and acted uncoordinated. Some acted as if they were more concerned with how their hair looked while performing the task. Younger girls ages 10 and under behaved differently. They put forth their best effort, showing what real running looks like, and pretended to throw a ball with real effort. When participants were asked if "like a girl" was an insult, most of them said yes. One of the younger girls said that it "sounds like you're trying to humiliate someone."[4] Always made the commercial to challenge the way boys and girls view being "like a girl." The company wants to help people understand that acting like a girl isn't bad as it is portrayed in gender stereotypes.

TEACHER BIASES

Teachers play an important role in either perpetuating the invisible bonds of male privilege in learning or cutting them. Research from the American Association of University Women shows that from preschool to college, males receive more attention from their teachers.

The term *gender domination* refers to boys dominating discussions and teachers recognizing boys more than girls in the classroom. A 1994 study found gender domination to be the most common form of sexism in coeducational schools. The study indicates that boys are more likely to call out answers than girls. However, when boys call out, teachers will listen. When girls call out, teachers are more likely to correct them and ask them to raise their hand to answer the question. The study points out that boys who receive higher grades receive about 25 percent of their teacher's attention.[5] The boys are given the opportunity to speak up and flourish in classroom settings. The girl with the highest grades in the classroom, however, is usually the one who receives the least amount of attention of all students in the class.

In 2009, the book *Still Failing at Fairness: How Gender Bias Cheats Girls and Boys in School and What We Can Do About It* backed up the previous studies. The authors observed public and private schools over several years and noted that teachers begin engaging less frequently with female students as early as elementary school, while engaging more with male students and providing them

MEDIA REPRESENTATION

Actress Geena Davis founded the Geena Davis Institute on Gender in Media. On her website, she provides lessons and teachers' guides. These can be used in classrooms to teach students about how the media normalizes things such as sexual harassment, bullying, body image, career choices for boys and girls, and other gender-related issues students face in schools. These resources challenge students to think about whether they believe the media is presenting the genders accurately and to think about the male and female genders from a different perspective than what is so commonly displayed on television, in film, and in social media. Too often, students are presented with limited materials that heavily favor the male gender, leaving girls out of the equation and giving the idea that girls are somehow less valuable and capable. The resources from the Geena Davis Institute can break those barriers and help students see through the negative connotations in order to recognize and appreciate all genders equally.

When some teachers realize they could be harming their female students' learning experience, they adjust their teaching methods.

with more feedback than the girls. The authors reported that after spending thousands of hours observing different classrooms and grade levels, they found that the time and attention of the teachers were unevenly distributed in favor of the boys.

Teachers tend to give boys more praise and constructive criticism, rewarding them for the substance of their work and encouraging them to find the answers when they are wrong. Girls, on the other hand, are praised more often for the quality of their penmanship or structure of their work, rather than given feedback on the substance of their work. When teachers were asked why the division of attention between boys and girls occurred, they often responded, "Boys have trouble reading, writing, doing math. They can't even sit still. They need me more."[6] This response captures a stereotype that because girls are quietly behaving well and learning on their own, they don't need extra help.

Today's schools reflect patriarchal views that revolve around male successes and encourage boys to be full participants in their education. Girls are treated in some cases like their education is less important than boys', and instead like they are distractions, rather than equal participants in their learning environment.

DISCUSSION STARTERS

- What examples of gender domination have you witnessed or experienced in your everyday life?
- How can teachers create a more equal learning environment for girls?
- Do you believe boys and girls are born with dominant skills, such as being good at math? Or are the skills learned? Support your reasoning.

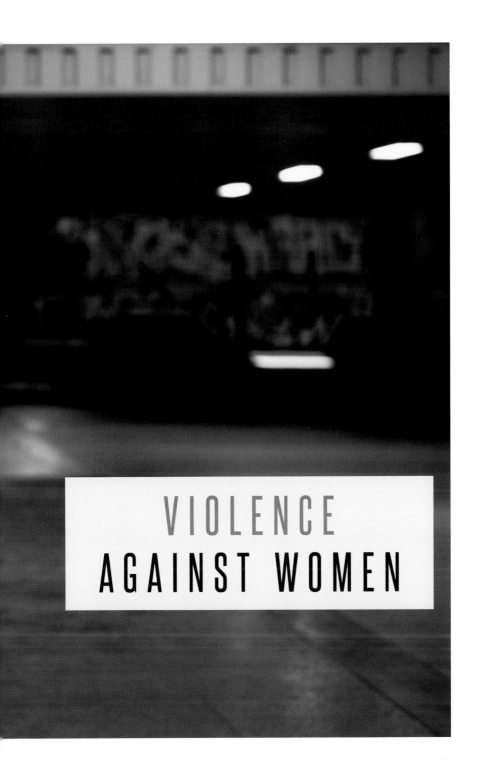

CHAPTER EIGHT

VIOLENCE
AGAINST WOMEN

Women are more likely than men to be victims of violent crimes, which often include sexual assault or rape. Transgender women of color are frequent targets of transgender violence. In 2016, nearly all of the transgender people killed were transgender women of color. Because men are perceived as larger, stronger, and more threatening, women are more frequent targets of assault. Men are much less likely to have to look over their shoulders walking to classes on college campuses or to their cars after a night out with friends. Men are still victims of crimes, but the type of victimization women experience is more often an assault on their bodies and is sexual in nature.

Women don't need to only fear assault from strangers on the street. Approximately 64 percent of rapes and sexual assaults against women were committed by someone they

GENDER-BASED VIOLENCE STATISTICS

The statistics surrounding crime and violence against girls and women are staggering. Approximately 83 percent of girls ages 12 to 16 in the United States have experienced sexual harassment in school.[1] One out of three high school girls will experience a violent dating relationship. Between 2004 and 2009, the portrayal of violence against girls and women on television increased 120 percent. Thirty-four percent of rape victims under age 18 are raped by a family member. And at least three women are killed by a spouse every day in the United States.[2] These are just some instances that show how prominent gender-based violence is in America.

knew. And almost 21 times more women than men reported being a victim of sexual assault or rape.[3]

Because of the rape culture and stigma in American society, it's believed that there are many more crimes of this nature that are not reported. Rape culture is operating when a woman tells someone she was raped and people question her: Were you drinking? What were you wearing? Did you do something to make him think you were interested? Questions like these indicate that the man is excused from being guilty of a crime against the woman and that the victim should be blamed instead. Today, when a woman accuses someone of rape or sexual assault, there is sometimes a level of mistrust. Often, she is assumed to have contributed to her assault in some way. This mind-set of putting the blame of the sexual assault on the victim perpetuates rape culture. Many girls and women are afraid of the criticism they'll experience if they come forward after an

WORKING TO PROTECT WOMEN

The Violence Against Women Act of 1994 (VAWA) categorizes rape as a hate crime based on gender. And while males get raped too, it is still considered a gender-based crime. This makes rape punishable under federal civil rights laws as well as state criminal statutes, so people who commit this type of crime will be subjected to harsher penalties. The VAWA increased penalties for violent crimes against women and provides funds to courts and police to provide protection for women.

assault. And if they don't report it, the male perpetrators remain free from punishment and can repeat the behavior.

HARASSMENT TOWARD WOMEN

It's not uncommon for women to receive hoots from men on the street, unwanted touching from classmates, and unprovoked comments from coworkers. Women's heightened sense of danger in these situations is a feeling that most men do not experience as frequently. Men are still targets and victims of harassment and violence, but the bulk of the danger falls on women.

A 2014 study by Stop Street Harassment, a website dedicated to ending street harassment of women and men—including lesbian, gay, bisexual, transgender, and questioning (LGBTQ) people—polled 2,000 people in the United States. Sixty-five percent of the women surveyed had been harassed on the street. Of all the women who responded, 23 percent had been touched in a sexual manner, 20 percent had been followed by someone, and 9 percent had been forced into a sexual situation against their will. Among the men who responded, 25 percent had experienced street harassment.[4] The most common form of harassment directed toward the men was homophobic slurs.

"No Catcalling" signs were placed around New York City in an effort to end street harassment.

In 2014, a 24-year-old woman, Shoshana B. Roberts, allowed a campaign aimed at ending street harassment to videotape her as she walked through New York City for ten hours. She wore jeans and a black crewneck shirt. As she silently walked down city sidewalks, she received demands such as "Smile!" and comments including "Hey, baby." Men also followed her down the sidewalk for minutes at a time. One man walked closely beside her and said, "You don't wanna talk? Because I'm ugly? Huh? We can't be friends? Nothing? You don't speak? If I give you my number, would you talk to me?" Others got irritated when Roberts remained silent. The video includes audio that says, "Hey what's up girl? How you doing?" When she ignored the comments, she was told, "Somebody's acknowledging you for being beautiful. You should say 'thank you' more!" The video claims that more than 100 instances of harassment took place within those 10 hours.[5]

ATTACKS THROUGH THE INTERNET

In 2014, Anita Sarkeesian, a feminist video game critic, canceled a lecture scheduled at Utah State University because someone sent an e-mail in which the sender threatened to carry out "the deadliest shooting in American history" if the event was not canceled.[6] The e-mail came from a student who claimed feminists had ruined his life and he wanted revenge.

But being the target for this type of violent threat wasn't new to Sarkeesian. She faces online harassment regularly for critiquing the way women are portrayed in video games. Sarkeesian hosts a web series called "Tropes vs. Women" in which she discusses the ways women are demeaned and mistreated in gaming. She points out that women are used by gaming characters as sexual playthings and are often the target of male violence. One example can be found in the game *Grand Theft Auto*, which allows players to have intimate relations with a female

The video game *Grand Theft Auto* is notorious for its demeaning depictions of women.

sex worker. When they are done, they have the option of beating her up and killing her.

Because of the popularity of Sarkeesian's web series, other gamers have threatened to kill her and her parents or to rape her to death. One gamer even created a video game called "Beat Up Anita Sarkeesian."

Sarkeesian and other game critics are not the only ones who deal with harassment. Everyday female gamers also deal with gender discrimination and harassment on a regular basis. Even though women make up approximately

48 percent of the gaming community, men continue to target them in acts of harassment. In fact, according to studies cited in Danielle Citron's book *Hate Crimes in CyberSpace*, 70 percent of women who participate in multiplayer games use male screen names to avoid harassment.[7]

Even when not playing video games, women and girls are harassed and stalked on the Internet, specifically in public forums and on social media platforms. In one survey of girls ages 10 to 17, one in five said they had been the target of unwanted sexual content online, ranging from suggestive comments to outright asking to meet for sex.[8] In addition, LGBTQ youth are three times more likely to be victims of online bullying compared with their straight peers.[9]

Female users also receive threats of rape and death from both strangers and people they know. A 2012 survey indicated 89 percent of domestic violence victims received threats of violence through technology, including cell phones and e-mail, also called cyberbullying

INTERNET BULLYING

Cyberbullying is a common form of bullying in which youth are harassed or threatened with violence through the Internet, phones, or social media. Cyberbullying includes things such as sending mean messages, spreading rumors online, stealing account information, and circulating pictures of people that are inappropriate or sexually explicit. Cyberbullying can cause teens serious problems, including depression, anxiety, and suicide.

or cyberstalking. According to the Justice Department, 80 percent of cyberstalkers are men, and 70 percent of the people being stalked online are women. The website Bullying Statistics reports that more than one-half of teens and adolescents have been bullied online or through their cell phones, and that only one out of every ten teenagers tells his or her parents about the cyberbullying.[10]

In today's society, male privilege allows men to treat people with disrespect and even become aggressive and violent without being fully held accountable for their actions. Women are suffering in public and in their own homes because of it.

DISCUSSION STARTERS

- What are some examples of harassment toward women you have either witnessed firsthand or heard about? How did bystanders react?

- How can authority figures begin to teach children to respect people regardless of their gender?

- Do you believe male violence against women is a learned behavior? Support your reasoning.

- What programs can be put in place to prevent cyberbullying and cyber attacks?

BROCK TURNER
CASE

On January 17, 2015, a group of students was having an on-campus party at Stanford University. That night, after meeting at the party, 19-year-old Brock Turner sexually assaulted Emily Doe (an assigned name used to protect her privacy). She was intoxicated and nearly unconscious when he removed her bra and underwear to assault her behind a dumpster in the dark. Two students saw the assault and noticed the girl was not moving. They approached Turner to ask what he was doing, and Turner attempted to run. The two men restrained Turner until the police arrived. The girl was alive but still not moving.

Turner was charged with sexual assault. He was attending Stanford on a swimming scholarship and showed potential in the sport. During the trial, friends and family praised Turner's character. His father complained that his son's life had been ruined over 20 minutes of activity, claiming Brock was so distraught he could hardly eat steak.

Turner was found guilty of three felony counts. His felonies could have given him a maximum of 14 years in prison, but Judge Aaron Persky handed him a 6-month sentence with 3 years of probation. Turner was released

Brock Turner claimed his unconscious victim consented to his sexual advances.

after serving only 3 months. In response to criticism of the lenient sentence, Judge Persky said, "A prison sentence would have a severe impact on him. I think he will not be a danger to others."[11] It is a clear case of male privilege when the impact of the attacker's punishment and the preservation of his character are more important than the impact on the victim.

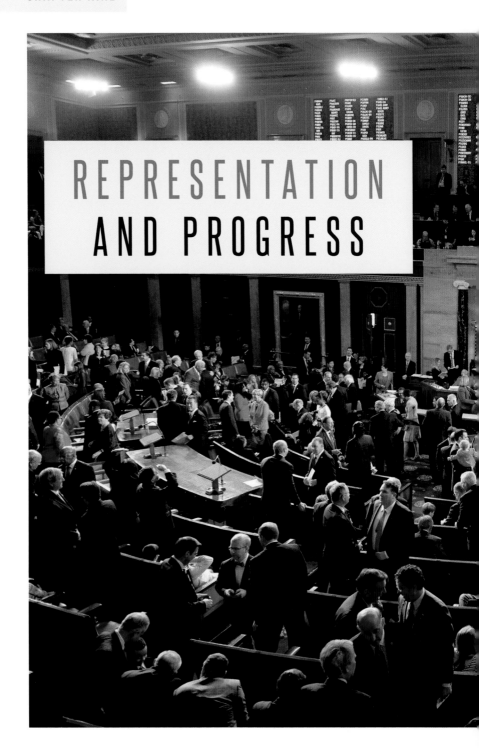

CHAPTER NINE

REPRESENTATION AND PROGRESS

Economists Justin Wolfers and Betsey Stevenson analyzed US citizens' happiness trends between 1970 and 2005. They found that in the 1970s, women rated their overall life satisfaction higher than men. During this time, women received more rights and financial power. In 1974, Congress passed legislation that outlawed credit discrimination based on marital status or sex. The next year, US states were prevented from denying women a seat on juries. In 1979, the first-ever conviction of spousal rape occurred, paving the way for legal changes to better protect women against assault.

The government has made progress in supporting women's rights. However, women remain underrepresented in the government in comparison with men. This remains true through all three branches of government. In 2017, only 105 women held seats in the US Congress, out of 535 members. Twenty-one of those women served in the Senate and 83 served in the House

A LOOK AT WOMEN IN GOVERNMENT

Since the beginning of the United States government, only 318 women have served in Congress. In 1916, Jeanette Rankin was the first woman to be elected to the House of Representatives. California has sent 41 women to Congress—more than any other state. New York comes in second place, having elected or appointed 28 women to Congress.[1] Neither Mississippi nor Vermont have ever elected a woman to hold a congressional seat.

of Representatives.[2] In the Supreme Court, three women sat on the bench in mid-2017. Out of 112 Supreme Court justices in history, only four had been women.[3] And there have been 45 male US presidents, but no woman has held the position. In fact, the 2016 presidential election was the first time that a woman, Hillary Clinton, won the nomination for a major political party. Clinton broke barriers for women in politics, but in the end she lost the presidency to Donald Trump.

In part, the number of women in political positions is low because women aren't getting put on the ballot. Professors Jennifer Lawless from American University and Richard Fox from Loyola Marymount University studied why women weren't running for office. They found that women are more likely to view the election process as biased against them, that women tend to think they aren't qualified to run for office, and that women have more responsibilities for household tasks and childcare than men.

The lack of representation of women in government positions impacts policies that affect women's everyday lives. With less than 20 percent of women making up the United States Congress, and only three women on the Supreme Court, women don't necessarily get an equal say in deciding what laws and restrictions should control them as a community or as individuals.[4] Research shows that female representatives are more likely than male ones to introduce legislation that relates to issues of importance to women. These issues include women's rights and family and children issues.

WOMEN'S HISTORY MONTH

In 1980, President Jimmy Carter proclaimed the week of March 8th National Women's History Week. March 8th had already been designated as International Women's Day, but activists wanted more than one day dedicated to the contributions of women. By 1987, most states had declared March Women's History Month, and Congress officially approved it. In his 1980 address to the nation, Carter said, "I urge libraries, schools, and community organizations to focus their observances on the leaders who struggled for equality— Susan B. Anthony, Sojourner Truth, Lucy Stone, Lucretia Mott, Elizabeth Cady Stanton, Harriet Tubman, and Alice Paul. Understanding the true history of our country will help us to comprehend the need for full equality under the law for all our people."[5]

WHAT ELSE CAN BE DONE TO ACHIEVE EQUALITY?

America has made great strides in addressing the unique issues women face. The Equal Pay Act was passed in 1963 to protect women from pay discrimination based on gender. While not effectively enforced, it makes it somewhat easier for women to pursue unfair wage claims. In 1972, Congress passed education amendments such as Title IX that prohibited gender-based discrimination in educational activities that are federally funded, meaning female sports teams and education programs must receive funding and equipment equal to male programs and sports. In 1994, the Violence Against Women Act was passed. The act provides funding for state programs to help women get out of domestic violence situations, as well as money for crisis centers, sexual assault hotlines, and women's shelters. It also provides protections for female students on college campuses.

Progress and advances have been made, but women are still underrepresented, oversexualized, and abused in American society. The media has saturated film, television, and the Internet with gore, rape, assault, and abuse.

MEN AGAINST SEXISM

The National Organization for Men Against Sexism (NOMAS) was established in 1981. The group has continued to support and defend women in their struggle for equality. NOMAS states that "whatever psychological burden men have to overcome, women are still the most universal and direct victims of our patriarchy. Our organization must take a highly visible and energetic position in support of women's struggle for equality. Our movement was born directly out of and continually nourished by feminism."[6] In the midst of a society that reflects male privilege, this group of men seeks to gain equality for women.

Because of this, many people have become detached and desensitized to the reality of how much they can hurt others. Male privilege, while often invisible to the eye, has great repercussions for other genders as they are undercut and imposed upon.

Activists across the country promote equal rights for all genders.

Everyday life in America, from pop culture and media to the education system, still reflects the control and perspective of the white men who created this country. As activists, educators, and lawmakers continue to work toward understanding how the bias in a male-dominated system alienates half the population of the country, the United States will grow into a more inclusive society that embraces all humans, regardless of gender.

DISCUSSION STARTERS

- In what ways can one person change the way women are represented in the government?

- What type of project or organization would you create to share the importance of gender equality?

- What type of progress do you hope to see in the near future to help improve the status of women? What can you do to help?

ESSENTIAL FACTS

SIGNIFICANT EVENTS

- The case of Brock Turner was a major moment spotlighting the existence of male privilege. Like Emily Doe, many girls and women who are assaulted or raped don't receive proper justice.

- The Lilly Ledbetter Fair Pay Restoration Act was approved by President Barack Obama in 2009. The new law allowed a worker to report unequal wages within 180 days of the last unequal paycheck, instead of the first unequal paycheck.

- President Donald Trump was elected in 2016 despite his history of sexism. During the month before the election, recordings were released of Trump talking with another man about the ways he has disrespectfully treated women.

KEY PLAYERS

- Jennifer Siebel Newsom is a writer, director, and producer of the film *Miss Representation*. Newsom shows startling statistics that support the evidence of male privilege. Her film focuses on the ways media, advertising, government, and education empower boys while teaching girls that they have only their looks and their bodies as keys to power and success.

- Geena Davis is a popular actress and founder of the Geena Davis Institute on Gender in Media. She uses her platform to educate others about the ways girls are underrepresented and demeaned in mainstream media and other areas. The website provides resources for research and educational materials that can be used by teachers in classroom environments to help students understand the current state of gender diversity and increase respect for all genders.

IMPACT ON SOCIETY

Male privilege is an invisible set of benefits favoring the male population of the United States. While some people argue that male privilege doesn't exist, there is evidence indicating there is a bias, even among women, that favors men and boys. Men, on average, receive more positive and rewarding attention and less criticism for their actions. This allows men—especially white men—to achieve higher status in education and the workplace even when their skills or experience are subpar in comparison with alternative candidates, including women and minorities.

QUOTE

"Privilege is when you think something is not a problem because it's not a problem to you personally. If you're part of a group that's being catered to, you believe that's the way it should be. 'It's always been that way, why would that be a problem for anyone?'"

—*David Gaider, author and former lead game developer for BioWare*

GLOSSARY

BIAS

Prejudice in favor of or against one thing, person, or group compared with another, usually in a way considered to be unfair.

DISCRIMINATION

Unfair treatment of other people, usually because of race, age, or gender.

FEMINISM

The belief that women should have the same opportunities and rights as men politically, socially, and economically.

FEMINIST

A person who supports the rights and progress of feminism and women in general.

PATRIARCHY

A system of beliefs that empowers men at the expense of women.

PRIVILEGE

A benefit, right, or immunity that is given to a specific group.

SEXISM

Discrimination or prejudice toward people based on their sex.

SEXUAL HARASSMENT

Unwanted physical or verbal sexual advances.

SEXUALIZE

To assign a sexual label or nature to something.

STEREOTYPE

A widely held but oversimplified idea about a particular type of person or thing.

SUBMISSIVE

Willing to yield or give in to others.

ADDITIONAL
RESOURCES

SELECTED BIBLIOGRAPHY

Doak, Melissa J. *Women in American Society*. Detroit, MI: Gale
   Cengage Learning, 2012. Print.

Johnson, Maisha Z. "160+ Examples of Male Privilege in All Areas of
   Life." *Everyday Feminism*. Everyday Feminism, 30 Jan. 2017. Web.
   3 May 2017.

McIntosh, Peggy. *White Privilege: Unpacking the Invisible Knapsack*.
   Philadelphia, PA: Peace and Freedom Magazine, 1989. Print.

FURTHER READINGS

Bialik, Mayim. *Girling Up: How to Be Strong, Smart and Spectacular*.
   New York: Philomel, 2017. Print.

Higgins, Melissa. *The Gender Wage Gap*. Minneapolis, MN: Abdo,
   2016. Print.

Noyce, Pendred. *Magnificent Minds: 16 Pioneering Women in Science
   & Medicine*. Boston, MA: Tumblehome Learning, 2015. Print.

ONLINE RESOURCES

Booklinks
NONFICTION NETWORK
FREE! ONLINE NONFICTION RESOURCES

To learn more about male privilege, visit **abdobooklinks.com**. These links are routinely monitored and updated to provide the most current information available.

MORE INFORMATION

For more information on this subject, contact or visit the following organizations:

HOLLABACK!
Local Chapters Nationwide
ihollaback.org

Hollaback! is a global movement to end harassment powered by a network of grassroots activists working together to understand harassment and ignite public conversations.

NATIONAL WOMEN'S HALL OF FAME
76 Fall Street
Seneca Falls, NY 13148
315-568-8060
womenofthehall.org

The National Women's Hall of Fame celebrates women who have made significant contributions to the community, to other women, and to the United States.

SOURCE NOTES

CHAPTER 1. WHAT IS MALE PRIVILEGE?

1. "The Declaration of Independence." *UShistory.org*. Independence Hall Association, n.d. Web. 18 Aug. 2017.

2. "Abigail Adams Remember the Ladies Letter 1776." *Hanover College*. Hanover College History Department, n.d. Web. 18 Aug. 2017.

3. Joshua Rothman. "The Origins of 'Privilege.'" *New Yorker*. Conde Nast, 12 May 2014. Web. 1 Sept. 2017.

4. "The Simple Truth about the Gender Pay Gap." *AAUW*. AAUW, n.d. Web. 18 Aug. 2017.

5. Nikita Redkar. "7 Reasons People Argue That Female Privilege Exists—And Why They're Mistaken." *Everyday Feminism*. Everyday Feminism, 25 Jan. 2016. Web. 18 Aug. 2017.

6. Tyler Wilde. "GDC 2013: BioWare's David Gaider Asks, 'How About We Just Decide How Not to Repel Women?'" *PC Gamer*. PC Gamer, 29 Mar. 2013. Web. 18 Aug. 2017.

CHAPTER 2. IT'S A MAN'S WORLD

1. "Stop Telling Women to Smile." *Stop Telling Women to Smile*. Tatyana Fazlalizadeh, n.d. Web. 18 Aug. 2017.

2. "Can an Angry Woman Get Ahead? Status Conferral, Gender, and Expression of Emotion in the Workplace." *Women and Public Policy Program*. President and Fellows of Harvard College, n.d. Web. 18 Aug. 2017.

3. Jonathan Martin, Maggie Haberman, and Alexander Burns. "Lewd Donald Trump Tape Is a Breaking Point for Many in the G.O.P." *New York Times*. New York Times, 8 Oct. 2016. Web. 18 Aug. 2017.

4. Elizabeth J Meyer. "The Danger of 'Boys Will Be Boys.'" *Psychology Today*. Sussex Publishers, 14 Mar. 2014. Web. 18 Aug. 2017.

5. "Robertson Letter Attacks Feminists." *New York Times*. New York Times, 25 Aug. 1992. Web. 18 Aug. 2017.

6. Andrew Good. "When It Comes to Women in Sports, TV News Tunes Out." *USC News*. University of Southern California, 5 June 2015. Web. 18 Aug. 2017.

7. Jennifer L. Knight and Traci A. Giuliano. "He's a Laker; She's a 'Looker': The Consequences of Gender-Stereotypical Portrayals of Male and Female Athletes by the Print Media." *Sex Roles* 45.3 (2001): 219. Print.

8. Shadia Duske. "Toxic Culture 101: Understanding the Sexualization of Women." *Ms. Magazine*. Ms. Magazine, 4 Jan. 2016. Web. 18 Aug. 2017.

CHAPTER 3. FREE SPEECH

1. Tonja Jacobi and Dylan Schweers. "Justice, Interrupted: The Effect of Gender, Ideology and Seniority at Supreme Court Oral Arguments." *Virginia Law Review* (forthcoming fall 2017): 8. Print.

2. "Language Myth #6." *PBS*. MacNeil/Lehrer Productions, n.d. Web. 21 Aug. 2017.

3. Rebecca Solnit. "Men Explain Things to Me." *Guernica*. Guernica, 20 Aug. 2012 Web. 21 Aug. 2017.

CHAPTER 4. PRIVILEGE IN THE WORKPLACE

1. Jeanne Sahadi. "Yes, Men Earn More Than Women. Except in These Jobs." *CNN*. Cable News Network, 23 Mar. 2016. Web. 15 Apr. 2017.

2. "Sexual Harassment Charges." *U.S. Equal Employment Opportunity Commission*. U.S. Equal Employment Opportunity Commission, n.d. Web. 21 Aug. 2017.

3. "Moving Women Forward." *Equal Rights Advocates*. Equal Rights Advocates, n.d. Web. 21 Aug. 2017.

4. "The Simple Truth about the Gender Pay Gap." *AAUW*. AAUW, n.d. Web. 21 Aug. 2017.

5. "What Is the Gender Pay Gap?" *PayScale*. PayScale, n.d. Web. 21 Aug. 2017.

6. Ibid.

7. Lisa Maatz and Anne Hedgepeth. "Women and Work: 50 Years of Change Since the American Women Report." *United States Department of Labor*. United States Department of Labor, n.d. Web. 6 Oct. 2017.

8. "Women in the Labor Force." *United States Department of Labor*. United States Department of Labor, n.d. Web. 21 Aug. 2017.

9. "The Lilly Ledbetter Fair Pay Act." *Lilly Ledbetter*. Lillyledbetter.com, n.d. Web. 21 Aug. 2017.

10. Rachel Gillett. "Hardly Any Women Made It to the 'Highest-Paid CEOs' List—But That's Just a Symptom of an Even Greater Problem." *Business Insider*. Business Insider, 26 May, 2017. Web. 21 Aug. 2017.

11. Melissa J. Doak. *Women in American Society*. Detroit MI: Gale, 2010. Print.

12. Joan C. Williams and Rachel Dempsey. *What Works for Women at Work*. New York: New York UP, 2014. Print.

CHAPTER 5. FAMILY AND RELATIONSHIPS

1. Kelley Holland. "Working Moms Still Take On Bulk of Household Chores." *CNBC*. CNBC, 28 Apr. 2015. Web. 22 Aug. 2017.

2. Ibid.

3. "Husbands Create 7 Hours of Extra Housework a Week: Study." *Reuters*. Reuters, 4 Apr. 2008. Web. 22 Aug. 2017.

4. "Women in the Labor Force." *United States Department of Labor*. United States Department of Labor, n.d. Web. 22 Aug. 2017.

5. "How Much You'll Spend on Childcare." *BabyCenter*. BabyCenter, n.d. Web. 22 Aug. 2017.

6. Liz Gumbinner. "The Myth of the Rich, Selfish Working Mom." *HuffPost*. Oath, 13 Apr. 2012. Web. 22 Aug. 2017.

7. Lawrence Mishel, Elise Gould, and Josh Bivens. "Wage Stagnation in Nine Charts." *Economic Policy Institute*. Economic Policy Institute, 16 Jan. 2015. Web. 22 Aug. 2017.

SOURCE NOTES
CONTINUED

8. Alexis Coe. "Dads Caring for Their Kids: It's Parenting, Not Babysitting." *Atlantic.* Atlantic Monthly Group, 23 Jan. 2013. Web. 22 Aug. 2017.

CHAPTER 6. HEALTH AND BODY IMAGE

1. "Body Image." *About-Face.* About-Face, n.d. Web. 22 Aug. 2017.

2. Ibid.

3. *Miss Representation.* Dir. Jennifer Siebel Newsom. Girls Club Entertainment, 2011. Netflix.

4. Megan Willett. "Here's Proof Women Pay More for the Same Products Men Buy." *Business Insider.* Business Insider, 24 Apr. 2015. Web. 22 Aug. 2017.

5. Elizabeth Narins. "10 Things That Cost More for Women." *Cosmopolitan.* Hearst Communications, 13 Mar. 2015. Web. 22 Aug. 2017.

6. Colleen Kratofil. "Can You Guess How Much a Woman Spends on Makeup in Her Lifetime?" *People.* Time, 30 Mar. 2017. Web. 12 Oct. 2017.

7. Joe Fassler. "How Doctors Take Women's Pain Less Seriously." *Atlantic.* Atlantic Monthly Group, 15 Oct. 2015. Web. 22 Aug. 2017.

8. "The Many Ways the American Health Care Act Would Jeopardize Women's Health and Economic Security." *National Women's Law Center.* NWLC, 24 May 2017. Web. 22 Aug. 2017.

9. Ibid.

10. Catherine New. "Health Care Costs Are Greater for Women in Most States." *HuffPost.* Oath, 19 Mar. 2012. Web. 23 Aug. 2017.

11. "The Many Ways the American Health Care Act Would Jeopardize Women's Health and Economic Security." *National Women's Law Center.* NWLC, 24 May 2017. Web. 22 Aug. 2017.

CHAPTER 7. PRIVILEGE IN EDUCATION

1. Kay A. Chick. "Gender Balance in K–12 American History Textbooks." *Social Studies Research and Practice* 1.3 (2006): 287. Web. 23 Aug. 2017.

2. Joan C. Williams. "The 5 Biases Pushing Women Out of STEM." *Harvard Business Review.* Harvard Business School Publishing, 24 Mar. 2015. Web. 23 Aug. 2017.

3. Rebecca Alber. "Gender Equity in the Classroom." *Edutopia.* George Lucas Educational Foundation, 27 Jan. 2017. Web. 23 Aug. 2017.

4. "#LikeAGirl: How It All Started." *Always.* Procter & Gamble, n.d. Web. 23 Aug. 2017.

5. "Gender Bias in the Classroom: How Teachers Exhibit and Perpetuate Sexism." *Gender Equity in the Classroom.* Hamilton College, n.d. Web. 23 Aug. 2017.

6. Ibid.

CHAPTER 8. VIOLENCE AGAINST WOMEN

1. "Fast Facts: Statistics on Violence against Women and Girls." *UN Women.* United Nations Entity for Gender Equality, n.d. Web. 23 Aug. 2017.

2. Soraya Chemaly. "50 Facts about Domestic Violence." *Joyful Heart Foundation.* Joyful Heart Foundation, 30 Nov. 2012. Web. 23 Aug. 2017.

3. Melissa J. Doak. *Women in American Society.* Detroit MI: Gale, 2010. Print.

4. "Statistics." *Stop Street Harassment.* Stop Street Harassment, n.d. Web. 23 Aug. 2017.

5. Rob Bliss Creative. "10 Hours of Walking in NYC as a Woman." *YouTube.* YouTube, 28 Oct. 2014. Web. 23 Aug. 2017.

6. Saeed Ahmed and Tony Marco. "Anita Sarkeesian Forced to Cancel Utah State Speech after Mass Shooting Threat." *CNN.* Cable News Network, 15 Oct. 2014. Web. 23 Aug. 2017.

7. Soraya Chemaly. "There's No Comparing Male and Female Harassment Online." *Time.* Time, 9 Sept. 2014. Web. 23 Aug. 2017.

8. "Online with a Sexual Predator." *ABC News.* ABC News Internet Ventures, n.d. Web. 23 Aug. 2017.

9. Soraya Chemaly. "There's No Comparing Male and Female Harassment Online." *Time.* Time, 9 Sept. 2014. Web. 23 Aug. 2017.

10. "Cyber Bullying Statistics." *Bullying Statistics.* Bullying Statistics, n.d. Web. 23 Aug. 2017.

11. Ashley Fantz. "Stanford Rape Case: Who Is the Judge Who Gave Brock Turner 6 Months?" *CNN.* Cable News Network, 9 June 2016. Web. 23 Aug. 2017.

CHAPTER 9. REPRESENTATION AND PROGRESS

1. "Women in the U.S. Congress 2017." *Center for American Women and Politics.* Center for American Women and Politics, n.d. Web. 23 Aug. 2017.

2. Ibid.

3. Tonja Jacobi and Dylan Schweers. "Legal Scholarship Highlight: Justice Interrupted—Gender, Ideology and Seniority at the Supreme Court." *Supreme Court of the United States Blog.* SCOTUSblog, 5 Apr. 2017. Web. 23 Aug. 2017.

4. "The Impact of Women in Elective Office." *Political Party.* Swanee Hunt, n.d. Web. 23 Aug. 2017.

5. Molly Murphy MacGregor. "Why March Is National Women's History Month." *National Women's History Project.* National Women's History Project, n.d. Web. 23 Aug. 2017.

6. "Tenets." *National Organization for Men against Sexism.* NOMAS, n.d. Web. 23 Aug. 2017.

INDEX

ABOUT THE AUTHORS

DUCHESS HARRIS, JD, PHD

Professor Harris is the chair of the American Studies Department at Macalester College. The author and coauthor of four books (*Hidden Human Computers: The Black Women of NASA* and *Black Lives Matter* with Sue Bradford Edwards, *Racially Writing the Republic: Racists, Race Rebels, and Transformations of American Identity* with Bruce Baum, and *Black Feminist Politics from Kennedy to Clinton/Obama*), she has been an associate editor for *Litigation News*, the American Bar Association Section's quarterly flagship publication, and was the first editor-in-chief of *Law Raza Journal*, an interactive online race and the law journal for William Mitchell College of Law.

She has earned a PhD in American Studies from the University of Minnesota and a Juris Doctorate from William Mitchell College of Law.

HEIDI DEAL

Heidi Deal spends her evenings writing books for children. When she's not writing, she's exploring nature on hiking adventures with her son and daughter or learning with them about history and science. The leaves of the trees and the pages of books inspire her to continue writing to share ideas.